New Poems by Robert Seymour Bridges

Robert Bridges was born in Walmer, Kent on the 23rd of October 1844. He went to study medicine intending to practice until the age of forty and then retire to write poetry.

Lung disease forced him to retire in 1882, and from that point on he devoted himself to writing and literary research. However, Bridges' literary work started long before his retirement, his first collection of poems having been published in 1873.

He was appointed Poet Laureate in 1913 by George V, the only medical graduate to have held the office.

He died in Oxford on the 21st of April 1930.

Index of Contents

BASIL AND EDWARD

Man hath with man on earth no holier bond
Than that the Muse weaves with her dreamy thread:
Nor e'er was such transcendent love more fond
Than that which Edward unto Basil led,
Wandering alone across the woody shires
To hear the living voice of that wide heart,
To see the eyes that read the world's desires,
And touch the hand that wrote the roving rhyme.
Diverse their lots as distant were their homes,
And since that early meeting, jealous Time
Knitting their loves had held their lives apart.

But now again were these fine lovers met
And sat together on a rocky hill
Looking upon the vales of Somerset,
Where the far sea gleam'd o'er the bosky combes,
Satisfying their spirits the livelong day
With various mirth and revelation due
And delicate intimacy of delight,
As there in happy indolence they lay
And drank the sun, while round the breezy height
Beneath their feet rabbit and listless ewe
Nibbled the scented herb and grass at will.

Much talked they at their ease; and at the last
Spoke Edward thus, "Twas on this very hill
This time of the year,—but now twelve years are past,—
That you provoked in verse my younger skill
To praise the months against your rival song;
And ere the sun had westered ten degrees
Our rhyme had brought him thro' the Zodiac.
Have you remembered?'—Basil answer'd back,
'Guest of my solace, how could I forget?
Years fly as months that seem'd in youth so long.
The precious life that, like indifferent gold,
Is disregarded in its worth to hold
Some jewel of love that God therein would set,
It passeth and is gone.'—'And yet not all,'
Edward replied: 'The passion as I please

Of that past day I can to-day recall;
And if but you, as I, remember yet
Your part thereof, and will again rehearse,
For half an hour we may old Time outwit.'
And Basil said, 'Alas for my poor verse!
What happy memory of it still endures
Will thank your love: I have forgotten it.
Speak you my stanzas, I will ransom yours.
Begin you then as I that day began,
And I will follow as your answers ran.'

JANUARY

EDWARD

The moon that mounts the sun's deserted way,
Turns the long winter night to a silver day;
But setteth golden in face of the solemn sight
Of her lord arising upon a world of white.

FEBRUARY

BASIL

I have in my heart a vision of spring begun
In a sheltering wood, that feels the kiss of the sun:
And a thrush adoreth the melting day that dies
In clouds of purple afloat upon saffron skies.

MARCH

EDWARD

ow carol the birds at dawn, and some new lay
Announceth a homecome voyager every day.
Beneath the tufted sallows the streamlet thrills
With the leaping trout and the gleam of the daffodils.

APRIL

BASIL

Then laugheth the year; with flowers the meads are bright;
The bursting branches are tipped with flames of light:
The landscape is light; the dark clouds flee above,
And the shades of the land are a blue that is deep as love.

MAY

EDWARD

But if you have seen a village all red and old
In cherry-orchards a-sprinkle with white and gold,
By a hawthorn seated, or a witch-elm flowering high,
A gay breeze making riot in the waving rye!

JUNE

BASIL

Then night retires from heaven; the high winds go
A-sailing in cloud-pavilions of cavern'd snow.
O June, sweet Philomel sang thy cradle-lay;
In rosy revel thy spirit shall pass away.

JULY

EDWARD

Heavy is the green of the fields, heavy the trees
With foliage hang, drowsy the hum of bees
In the thund'rous air: the crowded scents lie low:
Thro' tangle of weeds the river runneth slow.

AUGUST

BASIL

A reaper with dusty shoon and hat of straw
On the yellow field, his scythe in his armës braw:
Beneath the tall grey trees resting at noon
From sweat and swink with scythe and dusty shoon.

SEPTEMBER

EDWARD

Earth's flaunting flower of passion fadeth fair
To ripening fruit in sunlit veils of the air,
As the art of man makes wisdom to glorify
The beauty and love of life born else to die.

OCTOBER

BASIL

On frosty morns with the woods aflame, down, down
The golden spoils fall thick from the chestnut crown.
May Autumn in tranquil glory her riches spend,
With mellow apples her orchard-branches bend.

NOVEMBER

EDWARD

Sad mists have hid the sun, the land is forlorn:
The plough is afield, the hunter windeth his horn.
Dame Prudence looketh well to her winter stores,
And many a wise man finds his pleasure indoors.

DECEMBER

BASIL

I pray thee don thy jerkin of olden time,
Bring us good ice, and silver the trees with rime;
And I will good cheer, good music and wine bestow,
When the Christmas guest comes galloping over the snow.

Thus they in verse alternate sang the year
For rabbit shy and listless ewe to hear,
Among the grey rocks on the mountain green
Beneath the sky in fair and pastoral scene,
Like those Sicilian swains, whose doric tongue
After two thousand years is ever young,—
Sweet the pine's murmur, and, shepherd, sweet thy pipe,—
Or that which gentle Virgil, yet unripe,
Of Tityrus sang under the spreading beech
And gave to rustic clowns immortal speech,
By rocky fountain or on flowery mead
Bidding their idle flocks at will to feed,
While they, retreated to some bosky glade,
Together told their loves, and as they played
Sang what sweet thing soe'er the poet feigned:
But these were men when good Victoria reigned,
Poets themselves, who without shepherd gear
Each of his native fancy sang the year.

ECLOGUE II

GIOVANNI DUPRÈ

LAWRENCE AND RICHARD

LAWRENCE
Look down the river—against the western sky—
The Ponte Santa Trinità—what throng
Slowly trails o'er with waving banners high,
With foot and horse! Surely they bear along
The spoil of one whom Florence honoureth:
And hark! the drum, the trumpeting dismay,
The wail of the triumphal march of death.

RICHARD
'Twill be the funeral of Giovánn Duprè
Wending to Santa Croce. Let us go
And see what relic of old splendour cheers
The dying ritual.

LAWRENCE
They esteem him well
To lay his bones with Michael Angelo.
Who might he be?

RICHARD
He too a sculptor, one
Who left a work long to resist the years.

LAWRENCE
You make me question further.

RICHARD
I can tell
All as we walk. A poor woodcarver's son,
Prenticed to cut his father's rude designs
(We have it from himself), maker of shrines,
In his mean workshop in Siena dreamed;
And saw as gods the artists of the earth,
And long'd to stand on their immortal shore,
And be as they, who in his vision gleam'd,
Dowering the world with grace for evermore.
So, taxing rest and leisure to one aim,
The boy of single will and inbred skill
Rose step by step to academic fame.

LAWRENCE
Do I not know him then? His figures fill
The tympana o'er Santa Croce's gate;
In the museum too, his Cain, that stands
A left-handed discobolos....

RICHARD
So great
His vogue, that elder art of classic worth
Went to the wall to give his statues room;
And last—his country's praise could do no more—
He cut the stone that honoured good Cavour.

LAWRENCE
I have seen the things.

RICHARD
He, finding in his hands
His life-desire possest, fell not in gloom,
Nor froth'd in vanity: his Sabbath earn'd
He look'd to spend in meditative rest:
So laying chisel by, he took a pen
To tell his story to his countrymen,
And prove (he did it) that the flower of all,
Rarest to attain, is in the power of all.

LAWRENCE
Yet nought he ever made, that I have learn'd,
In wood or stone deserved, nay not his best,
The Greek or Tuscan name for beautiful.
'Twas level with its praise, had force to pull
Favour from fashion.

RICHARD
Yet he made one thing
Worthy of the lily city in her spring;
For while in vain the forms of beauty he aped,
A perfect spirit in himself he shaped;
And all his lifetime doing less than well
Where he profess'd nor doubted to excel,
Now, where he had no scholarship, but drew
His art from love, 'twas better than he knew:
And when he sat to write, lo! by him stood
The heavenly Muse, who smiles on all things good;
And for his truth's sake, for his stainless mind,
His homely love and faith, she now grew kind,
And changed the crown, that from the folk he got,
For her green laurel, and he knew it not.

LAWRENCE
Ah! Love of Beauty! This man then mistook
Ambition for her?

RICHARD
In simplicity
Erring he kept his truth; and in his book
The statue of his grace is fair to see.

LAWRENCE
Then buried with their great he well may be.

RICHARD
And number'd with the saints, not among them
Who painted saints. Join we his requiem.

ECLOGUE III

FOURTH OF JUNE AT ETON

RICHARD AND GODFREY

RICHARD
Beneath the wattled bank the eddies swarm
In wandering dimples o'er the shady pool:
The same their chase as when I was at school;
The same the music, where in shallows warm
The current, sunder'd by the bushy isles,
Returns to join the main, and struggles free
Above the willows, gurgling thro' the piles:
Nothing is changed, and yet how changed are we!
—What can bring Godfrey to the Muses' bower?

GODFREY
What but brings you? The festal day of the year;
To live in boyish memories for an hour;
See and be seen: tho' you come seldom here.

RICHARD
Dread of the pang it was, fear to behold
What once was all myself, that kept me away.

GODFREY
You miss new pleasures coveting the old.

RICHARD
They need have prudence, who in courage lack;
'Twas that I might go on I looked not back.

GODFREY

Of all our company he, who, we say,
Fruited the laughing flower of liberty!

RICHARD
Ah! had I my desire, so should it be.

GODFREY
Nay, but I know this melancholy mood;
'Twas your poetic fancy when a boy.

RICHARD
For Fancy cannot live on real food:
In youth she will despise familiar joy
To dwell in mournful shades; as they grow real,
Then buildeth she of joy her far ideal.

GODFREY
And so perverteth all. This stream to me
Sings, and in sunny ripples lingeringly
The water saith 'Ah me! where have I lept?
Into what garden of life? what banks are these,
What secret lawns, what ancient towers and trees?
Where the young sons of heav'n, with shouts of play
Or low delighted speech, welcome the day,
As if the poetry of the earth had slept
To wake in ecstasy. O stay me! alas!
Stay me, ye happy isles, ere that I pass
Without a memory on my sullen course
By the black city to the tossing seas!'

RICHARD
So might this old oak say 'My heart is sere;
With greater effort every year I force
My stubborn leafage: soon my branch will crack,
And I shall fall or perish in the wrack:
And here another tree its crown will rear,
And see for centuries the boys at play:
And 'neath its boughs, on some fine holiday,
Old men shall prate as these.' Come see the game.

GODFREY
Yes, if you will. 'Tis all one picture fair.

RICHARD
Made in a mirror, and who looketh there
Must see himself. Is not a dream the same?

GODFREY

Life is a dream.

RICHARD
And you, who say it, seem
Dreaming to speak to a phantom in a dream.

IV

ELEGY

THE SUMMER-HOUSE ON THE MOUND

How well my eyes remember the dim path!
My homing heart no happier playground hath.
I need not close my lids but it appears
Through the bewilderment of forty years
To tempt my feet, my childish feet, between
Its leafy walls, beneath its arching green;
Fairer than dream of sleep, than Hope more fair
Leading to dreamless sleep her sister Care.

There grew two fellow limes, two rising trees,
Shadowing the lawn, the summer haunt of bees,
Whose stems, engraved with many a russet scar
From the spear-hurlings of our mimic war,
Pillar'd the portico to that wide walk,
A mossy terrace of the native chalk
Fashion'd, that led thro' the dark shades around
Straight to the wooden temple on the mound.
There live the memories of my early days,
There still with childish heart my spirit plays;
Yea, terror-stricken by the fiend despair
When she hath fled me, I have found her there;
And there 'tis ever noon, and glad suns bring
Alternate days of summer and of spring,
With childish thought, and childish faces bright,
And all unknown save but the hour's delight.

High on the mound the ivied arbour stood,
A dome of straw upheld on rustic wood:
Hidden in fern the steps of the ascent,
Whereby unto the southern front we went,
And from the dark plantation climbing free,
Over a valley look'd out on the sea.
That sea is ever bright and blue, the sky
Serene and blue, and ever white ships lie
High on the horizon steadfast in full sail,

Or nearer in the roads pass within hail,
Of naked brigs and barques that windbound ride
At their taut cables heading to the tide.

There many an hour I have sat to watch; nay, now
The brazen disk is cold against my brow,
And in my sight a circle of the sea
Enlarged to swiftness, where the salt waves flee,
And ships in stately motion pass so near
That what I see is speaking to my ear:
I hear the waves dash and the tackle strain,
The canvas flap, the rattle of the chain
That runs out thro' the hawse, the clank of the winch
Winding the rusty cable inch by inch,
Till half I wonder if they have no care,
Those sailors, that my glass is brought to bear
On all their doings, if I vex them not
On every petty task of their rough lot
Prying and spying, searching every craft
From painted truck to gunnel, fore and aft,—
Thro' idle Sundays as I have watch'd them lean
Long hours upon the rail, or neath its screen
Prone on the deck to lie outstretch'd at length,
Sunk in renewal of their wearied strength.

But what a feast of joy to me, if some
Fast-sailing frigate to the Channel come
Back'd here her topsail, or brought gently up
Let from her bow the splashing anchor drop,
By faint contrary wind stay'd in her cruise,
The Phaethon or dancing Arethuse,
Or some immense three-decker of the line,
Romantic as the tale of Troy divine;
Ere yet our iron age had doom'd to fall
The towering freeboard of the wooden wall,
And for the engines of a mightier Mars
Clipp'd their wide wings, and dock'd their soaring spars.
The gale that in their tackle sang, the wave
That neath their gilded galleries dasht so brave
Lost then their merriment, nor look to play
With the heavy-hearted monsters of to-day.

One noon in March upon that anchoring ground
Came Napier's fleet unto the Baltic bound:
Cloudless the sky and calm and blue the sea,
As round Saint Margaret's cliff mysteriously,
Those murderous queens walking in Sabbath sleep
Glided in line upon the windless deep:

For in those days was first seen low and black
Beside the full-rigg'd mast the strange smoke-stack,
And neath their stern revolv'd the twisted fan.
Many I knew as soon as I might scan,
The heavy Royal George, the Acre bright,
The Hogue and Ajax, and could name aright
Others that I remember now no more;
But chief, her blue flag flying at the fore,
With fighting guns a hundred thirty and one,
The Admiral ship The Duke of Wellington,
Whereon sail'd George, who in her gig had flown
The silken ensign by our sisters sewn.
The iron Duke himself,—whose soldier fame
To England's proudest ship had given her name,
And whose white hairs in this my earliest scene
Had scarce more honour'd than accustom'd been,—
Was two years since to his last haven past:
I had seen his castle-flag to fall half-mast
One morn as I sat looking on the sea,
When thus all England's grief came first to me,
Who hold my childhood favour'd that I knew
So well the face that won at Waterloo.

But now 'tis other wars, and other men;—
The year that Napier sail'd, my years were ten—
Yea, and new homes and loves my heart hath found:
A priest has there usurped the ivied mound,
The bell that call'd to horse calls now to prayers,
And silent nuns tread the familiar stairs.
Within the peach-clad walls that old outlaw,
The Roman wolf, scratches with privy paw.

V

O Love, I complain,
Complain of thee often,
Because thou dost soften
My being to pain:

Thou makest me fear
The mind that createth,
That loves not nor hateth
In justice austere;
Who, ere he make one,
With millions toyeth,
And lightly destroyeth
Whate'er is begun.

An' wer't not for thee,
My glorious passion,
My heart I could fashion
To sternness, as he.

But thee, Love, he made
Lest man should defy him,
Connive and outvie him,
And not be afraid:

Nay, thee, Love, he gave
His terrors to cover,
And turn to a lover
His insolent slave.

VI

THE SOUTH WIND

The south wind rose at dusk of the winter day,
The warm breath of the western sea
Circling wrapp'd the isle with his cloke of cloud,
And it now reach'd even to me, at dusk of the day,
And moan'd in the branches aloud:
While here and there, in patches of dark space,
A star shone forth from its heavenly place,
As a spark that is borne in the smoky chase;
And, looking up, there fell on my face—
Could it be drops of rain
Soft as the wind, that fell on my face?
Gossamers light as threads of the summer dawn,
Suck'd by the sun from midmost calms of the main,
From groves of coral islands secretly drawn,
O'er half the round of earth to be driven,
Now to fall on my face
In silky skeins spun from the mists of heaven.

Who art thou, in wind and darkness and soft rain
Thyself that robest, that bendest in sighing pines
To whisper thy truth? that usest for signs
A hurried glimpse of the moon, the glance of a star
In the rifted sky?
Who art thou, that with thee I
Woo and am wooed?
That robing thyself in darkness and soft rain
Choosest my chosen solitude,

Coming so far
To tell thy secret again,
As a mother her child, in her folding arm
Of a winter night by a flickering fire,
Telleth the same tale o'er and o'er
With gentle voice, and I never tire,
So imperceptibly changeth the charm,
As Love on buried ecstasy buildeth his tower,
—Like as the stem that beareth the flower
By trembling is knit to power;—
Ah! long ago
In thy first rapture I renounced my lot,
The vanity, the despondency and the woe,
And seeking thee to know
Well was 't for me, and evermore
I am thine, I know not what.

For me thou seekest ever, me wondering a day
In the eternal alternations, me
Free for a stolen moment of chance
To dream a beautiful dream
In the everlasting dance
Of speechless worlds, the unsearchable scheme,
To me thou findest the way,
Me and whomsoe'er
I have found my dream to share
Still with thy charm encircling; even to-night
To me and my love in darkness and soft rain
Under the sighing pines thou comest again,
And staying our speech with mystery of delight,
Of the kiss that I give a wonder thou makest,
And the kiss that I take thou takest.

VII

I climb the mossy bank of the glade:
My love awaiteth me in the shade.

She holdeth a book that she never heedeth:
In Goddës work her spirit readeth.

She is all to me, and I to her:
When we embrace, the stars confer.

O my love, from beyond the sky
I am calling thy heart, and who but I?

Fresh as love is the breeze of June,
In the dappled shade of the summer noon.

Catullus, throwing his heart away,
Gave fewer kisses every day.

Heracleitus, spending his youth
In search of wisdom, had less of truth.

Flame of fire was the poet's desire:
The thinker found that life was fire.

O my love! my song is done:
My kiss hath both their fires in one.

VIII

To my love I whisper, and say
Knowest thou why I love thee?—Nay:
Nay, she saith; O tell me again.—

When in her ear the secret I tell,
She smileth with joy incredible—

Ha! she is vain—O nay—
Then tell us!—Nay, O nay.

But this is in my heart,
That Love is Nature's perfect art,
And man hath got his fancy hence,
To clothe his thought in forms of sense.

Fair are thy works, O man, and fair
Thy dreams of soul in garments rare,
Beautiful past compare,
Yea, godlike when thou hast the skill
To steal a stir of the heavenly thrill:

But O, have care, have care!
'Tis envious even to dare:
And many a fiend is watching well
To flush thy reed with the fire of hell.

IX

My delight and thy delight

Walking, like two angels white,
In the gardens of the night:

My desire and thy desire
Twining to a tongue of fire,
Leaping live, and laughing higher;
Thro' the everlasting strife
In the mystery of life.

Love, from whom the world begun,
Hath the secret of the sun.

Love can tell, and love alone,
Whence the million stars were strewn,
Why each atom knows its own,
How, in spite of woe and death,
Gay is life, and sweet is breath:

This he taught us, this we knew,
Happy in his science true,
Hand in hand as we stood
Neath the shadows of the wood,
Heart to heart as we lay
In the dawning of the day.

X

SEPTUAGESIMA

Now all the windows with frost are blinded,
As punctual day with greedy smile
Lifts like a Cyclops evil-minded
His ruddy eyeball over the isle.

In an hour 'tis paled, in an hour ascended
A dazzling light in the cloudless grey.
Steel is the ice; the snow unblended
Is trod to dust on the white highway.

The lambkins frisk; the shepherd is melting
Drink for the ewes with a fire of straw:
The red flames leap at the wild air pelting
Bitterly thro' the leafless shaw.

Around, from many a village steeple
The sabbath-bells hum over the snow:
I give a blessing to parson and people

Across the fields as away I go.

Over the hills and over the meadows
Gay is my way till day be done:
Blue as the heaven are all the shadows,
And every light is gold in the sun.

XI

The sea keeps not the Sabbath day,
His waves come rolling evermore;
His noisy toil grindeth the shore,
And all the cliff is drencht with spray.

Here as we sit, my love and I,
Under the pine upon the hill,
The sadness of the clouded sky,
The bitter wind, the gloomy roar,
The seamew's melancholy cry
With loving fancy suit but ill.

We talk of moons and cooling suns,
Of geologic time and tide,
The eternal sluggards that abide
While our fair love so swiftly runs,

Of nature that doth half consent
That man should guess her dreary scheme
Lest he should live too well content
In his fair house of mirth and dream:

Whose labour irks his ageing heart,
His heart that wearies of desire,
Being so fugitive a part
Of what so slowly must expire.

She in her agelong toil and care
Persistent, wearies not nor stays,
Mocking alike hope and despair.

—Ah, but she too can mock our praise,
Enchanted on her brighter days,

Days, that the thought of grief refuse,
Days that are one with human art,
Worthy of the Virgilian muse,
Fit for the gaiety of Mozart.

XII

Riding adown the country lanes
One day in spring,
Heavy at heart with all the pains
Of man's imagining:—

The mist was not yet melted quite
Into the sky:
The small round sun was dazzling white,
The merry larks sang high:

The grassy northern slopes were laid
In sparkling dew,
Out of the slow-retreating shade
Turning from sleep anew:

Deep in the sunny vale a burn
Ran with the lane,
O'erhung with ivy, moss and fern
It laughed in joyful strain:

And primroses shot long and lush
Their cluster'd cream;
Robin and wren and amorous thrush
Carol'd above the stream:

The stillness of the lenten air
Call'd into sound
The motions of all life that were
In field and farm around:

So fair it was, so sweet and bright,
The jocund Spring
Awoke in me the old delight
Of man's imagining,

Riding adown the country lanes:
The larks sang high.—
O heart! for all thy griefs and pains
Thou shalt be loth to die.

XIII

PATER FILIO

Sense with keenest edge unusèd,
Yet unsteel'd by scathing fire;
Lovely feet as yet unbruisèd
On the ways of dark desire;
Sweetest hope that lookest smiling
O'er the wilderness defiling!

Why such beauty, to be blighted
By the swarm of foul destruction?
Why such innocence delighted,
When sin stalks to thy seduction?
All the litanies e'er chaunted
Shall not keep thy faith undaunted.

I have pray'd the sainted Morning
To unclasp her hands to hold thee;
From resignful Eve's adorning
Stol'n a robe of peace to enfold thee;
With all charms of man's contriving
Arm'd thee for thy lonely striving.

Me too once unthinking Nature,
—Whence Love's timeless mockery took me,—
Fashion'd so divine a creature,
Yea, and like a beast forsook me.
I forgave, but tell the measure
Of her crime in thee, my treasure.

XIV

NOVEMBER

The lonely season in lonely lands, when fled
Are half the birds, and mists lie low, and the sun
Is rarely seen, nor strayeth far from his bed;
The short days pass unwelcomed one by one.

Out by the ricks the mantled engine stands
Crestfallen, deserted,—for now all hands
Are told to the plough,—and ere it is dawn appear
The teams following and crossing far and near,
As hour by hour they broaden the brown bands
Of the striped fields; and behind them firk and prance
The heavy rooks, and daws grey-pated dance:
As awhile, surmounting a crest, in sharp outline
(A miniature of toil, a gem's design,)

They are pictured, horses and men, or now near by
Above the lane they shout lifting the share,
By the trim hedgerow bloom'd with purple air;
Where, under the thorns, dead leaves in huddle lie
Packed by the gales of Autumn, and in and out
The small wrens glide
With a happy note of cheer,
And yellow amorets flutter above and about,
Gay, familiar in fear.

And now, if the night shall be cold, across the sky
Linnets and twites, in small flocks helter-skelter,
All the afternoon to the gardens fly,
From thistle-pastures hurrying to gain the shelter
Of American rhododendron or cherry-laurel:
And here and there, near chilly setting of sun,
In an isolated tree a congregation
Of starlings chatter and chide,
Thickset as summer leaves, in garrulous quarrel:
Suddenly they hush as one,—
The tree top springs,—
And off, with a whirr of wings,
They fly by the score
To the holly-thicket, and there with myriads more
Dispute for the roosts; and from the unseen nation
A babel of tongues, like running water unceasing,
Makes live the wood, the flocking cries increasing,
Wrangling discordantly, incessantly,
While falls the night on them self-occupied;
The long dark night, that lengthens slow,
Deepening with Winter to starve grass and tree,
And soon to bury in snow
The Earth, that, sleeping 'neath her frozen stole,
Shall dream a dream crept from the sunless pole
Of how her end shall be.

XV

WINTER NIGHTFALL

The day begins to droop,—
Its course is done:
But nothing tells the place
Of the setting sun.

The hazy darkness deepens,
And up the lane

You may hear, but cannot see,
The homing wain.

An engine pants and hums
In the farm hard by:
Its lowering smoke is lost
In the lowering sky.

The soaking branches drip,
And all night through
The dropping will not cease
In the avenue.

A tall man there in the house
Must keep his chair:
He knows he will never again
Breathe the spring air:

His heart is worn with work;
He is giddy and sick
If he rise to go as far
As the nearest rick:

He thinks of his morn of life,
His hale, strong years;
And braves as he may the night
Of darkness and tears.

XVI

Since we loved,—(the earth that shook
As we kissed, fresh beauty took)—
Love hath been as poets paint,
Life as heaven is to a saint;

All my joys my hope excel,
All my work hath prosper'd well,
All my songs have happy been,
O my love, my life, my queen.

XVII

When Death to either shall come,—
I pray it be first to me,—
Be happy as ever at home,
If so, as I wish, it be.

Possess thy heart, my own;
And sing to the child on thy knee,
Or read to thyself alone
The songs that I made for thee.

XVIII

WISHES

I wish'd to sing thy grace, but nought
Found upon earth that could compare:
Some day, maybe, in heaven, I thought,—
If I should win the welcome there,—

There might I make thee many a song:
But now it is enough to say
I ne'er have done our life the wrong
Of wishing for a happier day.

XIX

A LOVE LYRIC

Why art thou sad, my dearest?
What terror is it thou fearest,
Braver who art than I
The fiend to defy?

Why art thou sad, my dearest?
And why in tears appearest,
Closer than I that wert
At hiding thy hurt?

Why art thou sad, my dearest,
Since now my voice thou hearest?
Who with a kiss restore
Thy valour of yore.

XX

ΕΡΩΣ

Why hast thou nothing in thy face?
Thou idol of the human race,

Thou tyrant of the human heart,
The flower of lovely youth that art;
Yea, and that standest in thy youth
An image of eternal Truth,
With thy exuberant flesh so fair,
That only Pheidias might compare,
Ere from his chaste marmoreal form
Time had decayed the colours warm;
Like to his gods in thy proud dress,
Thy starry sheen of nakedness.

Surely thy body is thy mind,
For in thy face is nought to find,
Only thy soft unchristen'd smile,
That shadows neither love nor guile,
But shameless will and power immense,
In secret sensuous innocence.

O king of joy, what is thy thought?
I dream thou knowest it is nought,
And wouldst in darkness come, but thou
Makest the light where'er thou go.
Ah yet no victim of thy grace,
None who e'er long'd for thy embrace,
Hath cared to look upon thy face.

XXI

THE FAIR BRASS

An effigy of brass
Trodden by careless feet
Of worshippers that pass,
Beautiful and complete,

Lieth in the sombre aisle
Of this old church unwreckt,
And still from modern style
Shielded by kind neglect.

It shows a warrior arm'd:
Across his iron breast
His hands by death are charm'd
To leave his sword at rest,

Wherewith he led his men
O'ersea, and smote to hell

The astonisht Saracen,
Nor doubted he did well.

Would wé could teach our sons
His trust in face of doom,
Or give our bravest ones
A comparable tomb:

Such as to look on shrives
The heart of half its care;
So in each line survives
The spirit that made it fair;

So fair the characters,
With which the dusty scroll,
That tells his title, stirs
A requiem for his soul.

Yet dearer far to me,
And brave as he are they,
Who fight by land and sea
For England at this day;

Whose vile memorials,
In mournful marbles gilt,
Deface the beauteous walls
By growing glory built:

Heirs of our antique shrines,
Sires of our future fame,
Whose starry honour shines
In many a noble name

Across the deathful days,
Link'd in the brotherhood
That loves our country's praise,
And lives for heavenly good.

XXII

THE DUTEOUS HEART

Spirit of grace and beauty,
Whom men so much miscall:
Maidenly, modest duty,
I cry thee fair befall!

Pity for them that shun thee,
Sorrow for them that hate,
Glory, hath any won thee
To dwell in high estate!

But rather thou delightest
To walk in humble ways,
Keeping thy favour brightest
Uncrown'd by foolish praise;
In such retirement dwelling,
Where, hath the worldling been,
He straight returneth telling
Of sights that he hath seen,

Of simple men and truest
Faces of girl and boy;
The souls whom thou enduest
With gentle peace and joy.

Fair from my song befall thee,
Spirit of beauty and grace!
Men that so much miscall thee
Have never seen thy face.

XXIII

THE IDLE FLOWERS

I have sown upon the fields
Eyebright and Pimpernel,
And Pansy and Poppy-seed
Ripen'd and scatter'd well,

And silver Lady-smock
The meads with light to fill,
Cowslip and Buttercup,
Daisy and Daffodil;

King-cup and Fleur-de-lys
Upon the marsh to meet
With Comfrey, Watermint,
Loose-strife and Meadowsweet;

And all along the stream
My care hath not forgot
Crowfoot's white galaxy
And love's Forget-me-not:

And where high grasses wave
Shall great Moon-daisies blink,
With Rattle and Sorrel sharp
And Robin's ragged pink.

Thick on the woodland floor
Gay company shall be,
Primrose and Hyacinth
And frail Anemone,

Perennial Strawberry-bloom,
Woodsorrel's pencilled veil,
Dishevel'd Willow-weed
And Orchis purple and pale,

Bugle, that blushes blue,
And Woodruff's snowy gem,
Proud Foxglove's finger-bells
And Spurge with milky stem.

High on the downs so bare,
Where thou dost love to climb,
Pink Thrift and Milkwort are,
Lotus and scented Thyme;

And in the shady lanes
Bold Arum's hood of green,
Herb Robert, Violet,
Starwort and Celandine;

And by the dusty road
Bedstraw and Mullein tall,
With red Valerian
And Toadflax on the wall,

Yarrow and Chicory,
That hath for hue no like,
Silene and Mallow mild
And Agrimony's spike,
Blue-eyed Veronicas
And grey-faced Scabious
And downy Silverweed
And striped Convolvulus:

Harebell shall haunt the banks,
And thro' the hedgerow peer
Withwind and Snapdragon

And Nightshade's flower of fear.

And where men never sow,
Have I my Thistles set,
Ragwort and stiff Wormwood
And straggling Mignonette,

Bugloss and Burdock rank
And prickly Teasel high,
With Umbels yellow and white,
That come to kexes dry.

Pale Chlora shalt thou find,
Sun-loving Centaury,
Cranesbill and Sinjunwort,
Cinquefoil and Betony:

Shock-headed Dandelion,
That drank the fire of the sun:
Hawkweed and Marigold,
Cornflower and Campion.

Let Oak and Ash grow strong,
Let Beech her branches spread;
Let Grass and Barley throng
And waving Wheat for bread;

Be share and sickle bright
To labour at all hours;
For thee and thy delight
I have made the idle flowers.

But now 'tis Winter, child,
And bitter northwinds blow,
The ways are wet and wild,
The land is laid in snow.

XXIV

DUNSTONE HILL

A cottage built of native stone
Stands on the mountain-moor alone,
High from man's dwelling on the wide
And solitary mountain-side,

The purple mountain-side, where all

The dewy night the meteors fall,
And the pale stars musically set
To the watery bells of the rivulet,

And all day long, purple and dun,
The vast moors stretch beneath the sun,
The wide wind passeth fresh and hale,
And whirring grouse and blackcock sail.

Ah, heavenly Peace, where dost thou dwell?
Surely 'twas here thou hadst a cell,
Till flaming Love, wandering astray
With fury and blood, drove thee away.—

Far down across the valley deep
The town is hid in smoky sleep,
At moonless nightfall wakening slow
Upon the dark with lurid glow:

Beyond, afar the widening view
Merges into the soften'd blue,
Cornfield and forest, hill and stream,
Fair England in her pastoral dream.

To one who looketh from this hill
Life seems asleep, all is so still:
Nought passeth save the travelling shade
Of clouds on high that float and fade:

Nor since this landscape saw the sun
Might other motion o'er it run,
Till to man's scheming heart it came
To make a steed of steel and flame.

Him may you mark in every vale
Moving beneath his fleecy trail,
And tell whene'er the motions die
Where every town and hamlet lie.

He gives the distance life to-day,
Rushing upon his level'd way
From man's abode to man's abode,
And mocks the Roman's vaunted road,

Which o'er the moor purple and dun
Still wanders white beneath the sun,
Deserted now of men and lone
Save for this cot of native stone.

There ever by the whiten'd wall
Standeth a maiden fair and tall,
And all day long in vacant dream
Watcheth afar the flying steam.

SCREAMING TARN

The saddest place that e'er I saw
Is the deep tarn above the inn
That crowns the mountain-road, whereby
One southward bound his way must win.

Sunk on the table of the ridge
From its deep shores is nought to see:
The unresting wind lashes and chills
Its shivering ripples ceaselessly.

Three sides 'tis banked with stones aslant,
And down the fourth the rushes grow,
And yellow sedge fringing the edge
With lengthen'd image all arow.

'Tis square and black, and on its face
When noon is still, the mirror'd sky
Looks dark and further from the earth
Than when you gaze at it on high.

At mid of night, if one be there,
—So say the people of the hill—
A fearful shriek of death is heard,
One sudden scream both loud and shrill.

And some have seen on stilly nights,
And when the moon was clear and round,
Bubbles which to the surface swam
And burst as if they held the sound.—

'Twas in the days ere hapless Charles
Losing his crown had lost his head,
This tale is told of him who kept
The inn upon the watershed:

He was a lowbred ruin'd man
Whom lawless times set free from fear:

One evening to his house there rode
A young and gentle cavalier.

With curling hair and linen fair
And jewel-hilted sword he went;
The horse he rode he had ridden far,
And he was with his journey spent.

He asked a lodging for the night,
His valise from his steed unbound,
He let none bear it but himself
And set it by him on the ground.

'Here's gold or jewels,' thought the host,
'That's carrying south to find the king.'
He chattered many a loyal word,
And scraps of royal airs gan sing.

His guest thereat grew more at ease
And o'er his wine he gave a toast,
But little ate, and to his room
Carried his sack behind the host.

'Now rest you well,' the host he said,
But of his wish the word fell wide;
Nor did he now forget his son
Who fell in fight by Cromwell's side.

Revenge and poverty have brought
Full gentler heart than his to crime;
And he was one by nature rude,
Born to foul deeds at any time.

With unshod feet at dead of night
In stealth he to the guest-room crept,
Lantern and dagger in his hand,
And stabbed his victim while he slept.

But as he struck a scream there came,
A fearful scream so loud and shrill:
He whelm'd the face with pillows o'er,
And lean'd till all had long been still.

Then to the face the flame he held
To see there should no life remain:—
When lo! his brutal heart was quell'd:
'Twas a fair woman he had slain.

The tan upon her face was paint,
The manly hair was torn away,
Soft was the breast that he had pierced;
Beautiful in her death she lay.

His was no heart to faint at crime,
Tho' half he wished the deed undone.
He pulled the valise from the bed
To find what booty he had won.

He cut the straps, and pushed within
His murderous fingers to their theft.
A deathly sweat came o'er his brow,
He had no sense nor meaning left.

He touched not gold, it was not cold,
It was not hard, it felt like flesh.
He drew out by the curling hair
A young man's head, and murder'd fresh;

A young man's head, cut by the neck.
But what was dreader still to see,
Her whom he had slain he saw again,
The twain were like as like can be.

Brother and sister if they were,
Both in one shroud they now were wound,—
Across his back and down the stair,
Out of the house without a sound.

He made his way unto the tarn,
The night was dark and still and dank;
The ripple chuckling neath the boat
Laughed as he drew it to the bank.

Upon the bottom of the boat
He laid his burden flat and low,
And on them laid the square sandstones
That round about the margin go.

Stone upon stone he weighed them down,
Until the boat would hold no more;
The freeboard now was scarce an inch:
He stripp'd his clothes and push'd from shore.

All naked to the middle pool
He swam behind in the dark night;
And there he let the water in

And sank his terror out of sight.

He swam ashore, and donn'd his dress,
And scraped his bloody fingers clean;
Ran home and on his victim's steed
Mounted, and never more was seen.

But to a comrade ere he died
He told his story guess'd of none:
So from his lips the crime returned
To haunt the spot where it was done.

XXVI

THE ISLE OF ACHILLES

(FROM THE GREEK)

Τὸν φίλτατόν σοι παῖδ' ἐμοί τ', Ἀχιλλέα
ὑψει δύμους ναίοντα νησιωτικούς
Δευκήν κατ' ἀκτήν ἐντὸς Εὐξείνου πόρου.
Eur. And. 1250.

Voyaging northwards by the western strand
Of the Euxine sea we came to where the land
Sinks low in salt morass and wooded plain:
Here mighty Ister pushes to the main,
Forking his turbid flood in channels three
To plough the sands wherewith he chokes the sea.

Against his middle arm, not many a mile
In the offing of black water is the isle
Named of Achilles, or as Leukê known,
Which tender Thetis, counselling alone
With her wise sire beneath the ocean-wave
Unto her child's departed spirit gave,
Where he might still his love and fame enjoy,
Through the vain Danaan cause fordone at Troy.
Thither Achilles passed, and long fulfill'd
His earthly lot, as the high gods had will'd,
Far from the rivalries of men, from strife,
From arms, from woman's love and toil of life.
Now of his lone abode I will unfold
What there I saw, or was by others told.

There is in truth a temple on the isle;
Therein a wooden statue of rude style

And workmanship antique with helm of lead:
Else all is desert, uninhabited;
Only a few goats browse the wind-swept rocks,
And oft the stragglers of their starving flocks
Are caught and sacrificed by whomsoe'er,
Whoever of chance or purpose hither fare:
About the fence lie strewn their bleaching bones.

But in the temple jewels and precious stones,
Upheapt with golden rings and vials lie,
Thankofferings to Achilles, and thereby,
Written or scratch'd upon the walls in view,
Inscriptions, with the givers' names thereto,
Some in Romaic character, some Greek,
As each man in the tongue that he might speak
Wrote verse of praise, or prayer for good to come,
To Achilles most, but to Patroclus some;
For those who strongly would Achilles move
Approach him by the pathway of his love.

Thousands of birds frequent the sheltering shrine,
The dippers and the swimmers of the brine,
Sea-mew and gull and diving cormorant,
Fishers that on the high cliff make their haunt
Sheer inaccessible, and sun themselves
Huddled arow upon the narrow shelves:—
And surely no like wonder e'er hath been
As that such birds should keep the temple clean;
But thus they do: at earliest dawn of day
They flock to sea and in the waters play,
And when they well have wet their plumage light,
Back to the sanctuary they take flight
Splashing the walls and columns with fresh brine,
Till all the stone doth fairly drip and shine,
When off again they skim asea for more
And soon returning sprinkle steps and floor,
And sweep all cleanly with their wide-spread wings.

From other men I have learnt further things.
If any of free purpose, thus they tell,
Sail'd hither to consult the oracle,—
For oracle there was,—they sacrificed
Such victims as they brought, if such sufficed,
And some they slew, some to the god set free:
But they who driven from their course at sea
Chanced on the isle, took of the goats thereon
And pray'd Achilles to accept his own.
Then made they a gift, and when they had offer'd once,

If to their question there was no response,
They added to the gift and asked again;
Yea twice and more, until the god should deign
Answer to give, their offering they renew'd;
Whereby great riches to the shrine ensued.
And when both sacrifice and gifts were made
They worship'd at the shrine, and as they pray'd
Sailors aver that often hath been seen
A man like to a god, of warrior mien,
A beauteous form of figure swift and strong;
Down on his shoulders his light hair hung long
And his full armour was enchast with gold:
While some, who with their eyes might nought behold,
Say that with music strange the air was stir'd;
And some there are, who have both seen and heard:
And if a man wish to be favour'd more,
He need but spend one night upon the shore;
To him in sleep Achilles will appear
And lead him to his tent, and with good cheer
Show him all friendliness that men desire;
Patroclus pours the wine, and he his lyre
Takes from the pole and plays the strains thereon
Which Cheiron taught him first on Pelion.

These things I tell as they were told to me,
Nor do I question but it well may be:
For sure I am that, if man ever was,
Achilles was a hero, both because
Of his high birth and beauty, his country's call,
His valour of soul, his early death withal,
For Homer's praise, the crown of human art;
And that above all praise he had at heart
A gentler passion in her sovran sway,
And when his love died threw his life away.

XXVII

AN ANNIVERSARY

HE
Bright, my belovèd, be thy day,
This eve of Summer's fall:
And Autumn mass his flowers gay
To crown thy festival!

SHE
I care not if the morn be bright,

Living in thy love-rays:
No flower I need for my delight,
Being crownèd with thy praise.

HE
O many years and joyfully
This sun to thee return;
Ever all men speak well of thee,
Nor any angel mourn!

SHE
For length of life I would not pray,
If thy life were to seek;
Nor ask what men and angels say
But when of thee they speak.

HE
Arise! The sky hath heard my song,
The flowers o'erhear thy praise;
And little loves are waking long
To wish thee happy days.

XXVIII

REGINA CARA

JUBILEE-SONG, FOR MUSIC, 1897

Hark! The world is full of thy praise,
England's Queen of many days;
Who, knowing how to rule the free,
Hast given a crown to monarchy.

Honour, Truth and growing Peace
Follow Britannia's wide increase,
And Nature yield her strength unknown
To the wisdom born beneath thy throne!

In wisdom and love firm is thy fame:
Enemies bow to revere thy name:
The world shall never tire to tell
Praise of the queen that reignèd well.

O FELIX ANIMA, DOMINA PRAECLARA,
AMORE SEMPER CORONABERE
REGINA CARA.

Robert Seymour Bridges – A Short Biography

Robert Seymour Bridges, OM was born on 23 October 1844 at Walmer in Kent where he spent his early childhood in a house overlooking the anchoring ground of the British fleet. He was the fourth son and eighth child of John Thomas Bridges (1805–1853) and Harriett Elizabeth Affleck (1807–1897).

His father died at the age of only 47 in 1853 and a year later his mother remarried and the family relocated to Rochdale, where his stepfather, John Edward Nassau Molesworth, was the vicar.

In 1854 Bridges was sent to the elite public school of Eton College and attended there until 1863. Whilst there he met the poet Digby Mackworth Dolben and Lionel Muirhead, who became a lifelong friend.

After Eton he went to Oxford and the Corpus Christi College. Whilst studying he became good friends with Gerald Manley Hopkins. Hopkins is now considered the superior poet and Bridges probably knew this or at least was a great admirer as he was essential in ensuring the publication of the complete works of Hopkins in 1918. His edition of Hopkins's poems is considered a major contribution to English literature.

He received his degree and graduated from Oxford in 1867 with a second class in literae humaniores. His initial thought was to enter religious life with the Church of England and he travelled to the Middle East in furtherance of his knowledge on the subject. But instead he decided that life as a physician would be a better path and after learning German for eight months in Germany (that being the language of many scientific papers at the time) he began his study of medicine at St. Bartholomew's Hospital in 1869. His long term hope was that by the age of forty he could retire from medicine to devote himself to writing.

Bridges failed his final medical examinations in 1873 and as unable to immediately retake the papers, spent six months in Italy learning Italian and as much as he could about Italian art. In July 1874 he went to study medicine in Dublin. Re-examined in December of that year, he obtained his MB and became a house physician to Dr Patrick Black at St Bartholomew's Hospital.

He practiced as a casualty physician at this teaching hospital where he also engaged in a series of highly critical remarks about the Victorian medical establishment. Such was his workload that he claimed that whilst working as a young doctor he saw a staggering 30,940 patients in one year.

After being a house physician at St Bartholomew's he later became casualty physician and later assistant physician at the Hospital for Sick Children, Great Ormond Street, and then physician at Great Northern Hospital, Holloway.

A bout of severe pneumonia and lung disease forced his retirement from the medical profession in 1882 and so slightly ahead of schedule he began his literary career in earnest.

However he had, prior to this, been writing for several years. His first collection of poems having been published in 1873. Indeed its worth pointing out that his early materials were published privately, mainly to be given away to friends and his small circle of admirers as they sold little. It took Bridges some time to gain traction and a wider audience.

After his illness and a trip to Italy with Muirhead, Bridges moved with his mother to Yattendon in Berkshire.

It was during his residence in Yattendon, from 1882 to 1904, that Bridges wrote most of his best-known lyrics as well as eight plays and two masques, all in verse.

It was here that he first met and then in 1884 he married Monica Waterhouse, daughter of Alfred Waterhouse R.A., the famous architect. The couple had three children: Elizabeth (1887–1977), Margaret (1889–1926), and Edward Ettingdene Bridges (1892–1969). They would spend the rest of their lives in rural seclusion, in an idyllic marriage, first at Yattendon, Berkshire, then later at Boars Hill, Oxford

Bridges made an important contribution to hymnody with the publication in 1899 of his Yattendon Hymnal, which he created specifically for musical reasons. This collection of hymns, although not a financial success, became a bridge between the Victorian hymnody of the last half of the 19th century and the modern hymnody of the early 20th century. He was a chorister at Yattendon church for 18 years.

In 1902 Monica and his daughter Margaret became seriously ill with tuberculosis, and a move from Yattendon to a healthier climate was in order.

After living in several temporary homes they moved abroad to spend a year in Switzerland, and finally returning settled again in England at Chilswell House, which Bridges had designed and which was built on Boar's Hill overlooking Oxford University.

Bridges was elected to the Fellowship of the Royal College of Physicians of London in 1900.

His greatest achievement though was still some years ahead of him. The office of Poet Laureate was held by Alfred Austin but with his death it was offered first to Rudyard Kipling, who refused it, and thence to Bridges. He was appointed Poet Laureate in 1913 by George V, the only medical graduate to have ever held the office. It seems a strange choice given the 'write to order' brief of Poet Laureate but Bridges accepted and must have known of the strictures.

That same year along with Henry Bradley and Walter Raleigh he founded the Society for Pure English.

Bridges received advice from the young phonetician David Abercrombie on the reformed spelling system he was devising for the publication of his collected essays (later published in seven volumes by Oxford University Press, with the help of the distinguished typographer Stanley Morison, who designed the new letters). Thus Robert Bridges contributed to phonetics.

The office of Poet Laureate has been held by many great and well known poets such as John Dryden, William Wordsworth and Alfred Lord Tennyson.

Bridges at this stage was not highly regarded nor well known but more a safe pair of hands in a World rapidly being overshadowed by the storms about to erupt over Europe and the First World War.

The events of the First World War, including the wounding of his son, Edward, had a sobering effect on Bridges' poetry. He composed fiercely patriotic poems and letters, and in 1915 edited a volume of prose and poetry, The Spirit of Man, intended to appeal to readers living in war times.

One area where his work did resonate though was with a great many composers and specifically British. Many set his poetry to music and among them were Hubert Parry, Gustav Holst and Gerald Finzi.

Despite being made poet laureate Bridges was never a very well-known poet and only achieved his great popularity shortly before his death with The Testament of Beauty.

His best-known poems are found in the two earlier volumes of Shorter Poems (1890, 1894). His talents did not stop at poetry and his works include verse plays and literary criticism, including a study of the work of fellow poet John Keats.

As a poet Bridges stands rather apart from the tide of modern English verse, but his work has had great influence in a select circle, by its restraint, purity, precision, and delicacy yet strength of expression. It embodies a distinct theory of prosody. Bridges' deep faith underpinned much of his work.

In the book Milton's Prosody, he took an empirical approach to examining Milton's use of blank verse, and developed the somewhat controversial theory that Milton's practice was essentially syllabic. He considered free verse to be too limiting, and explained his position in the essay "Humdrum and Harum-Scarum".

Bridge's own efforts to "free" verse resulted in the poems he called "Neo-Miltonic Syllabics", which were collected in New Verse (1925). The metre of these poems was based on syllables rather than accents, and he used the principle again in the long philosophical poem The Testament of Beauty (1929), for which he received the Order of Merit. Perhaps The Testament of Beauty is his most highly regarded work but he also wrote and also translated historic hymns, and many of these were included in Songs of Syon (1904) and the later English Hymnal (1906). Several of Bridges' hymns and translations are still in use today.

Bridges work with the Society for Pure English (S.P.E.) was interrupted by the War but resumed in 1919. The work for the S.P.E. led to Bridges' only trip to America in 1924, during which he increased interest in the group among American scholars.

As previously mentioned his masterpiece, a long philosophical poem entitled The Testament of Beauty, was begun on Christmas Day, 1924, with fourteen lines of what he referred to as "loose Alexandrines." He set the piece aside until 1926, when the death of his daughter Margaret prompted him to resume work as a way to ease his grief. The Testament of Beauty was published in October 1929, one day after his eighty-fifth birthday and six months before his death.

A Victorian who by choice remained apart from the aesthetic movements of his day, Robert Bridges was a classicist and experimented with eighteenth-century classical forms..

On December 2nd 1929 he was pictured on the cover that week of Time Magazine

Robert Seymour Bridges' health was failing and undermined by cancer and its complications he died at his home, Chilswell, on 21 April 1930. His ashes are buried near the family cross in the churchyard of St Peter and St Paul's Church, Yattendon, Berkshire.

The cross was originally erected by Bridges in memory of his mother Harriet Elizabeth. There is also a memorial tablet to him inside the church.

Robert Seymour Bridges – A Concise Bibliography

Poetry collections
The Growth of Love (1876; 1889; 1898), a sequence of (24; 79; 69) sonnets
Prometheus the Firegiver: A Mask in the Greek Manner (1883)
Eros and Psyche: A Narrative Poem in Twelve Measures (1885; 1894), a story from the Latin of Apuleius
Shorter Poems, Books I–IV (1890)
Shorter Poems, Books I–V (1894)
New Poems (1899)
Demeter: A Mask (1905), performed 1904
Ibant Obscuri: An Experiment in the Classical Hexameter (1916), with reprint of summary of Stone's Prosody, accompanied by 'later observations & modifications'
October and Other Poems (1920)
The Tapestry: Poems (1925), in neo-Miltonic syllabics
New Verse (1926),
The Testament of Beauty (1929)

Verse drama
Nero (1885), historical tragedy; called The First Part of Nero after the publication of Nero: Part II
The Feast of Bacchus (1889); partly translated from the Heauton-Timoroumenos of Terence
Achilles in Scyros (1890), a drama in a mixed manner
Palicio (1890), a romantic drama in five acts in the Elizabethan manner
The Return of Ulysses (1890), a drama in five acts in a mixed manner
The Christian Captives (1890), a tragedy in five acts in a mixed manner; on the same subject as Calderón's El Principe Constante
The Humours of the Court (1893), a comedy in three acts; founded on Calderón's El secreto á voces and on Lope de Vega's El Perro del hortelano
Nero, Part II (1894)

Prose
Milton's Prosody, With a Chapter on Accentual Verse (1893; 1901; 1921), based on essays published in 1887 and 1889
Keats (1895)
Hymns from the Yattendon Hymnal (1899)
The Spirit of Man (1916)
Poems of Gerard Manley Hopkins (1918), edited with notes by R.B.
The Necessity of Poetry (1918)
Collected Essays, Papers, Etc. (1927–36)

www.ingramcontent.com/pod-product-compliance
Lightning Source LLC
Chambersburg PA
CBHW060102050426
42448CB00011B/2589